Travelling SOLO to Italy

Italy

Written and illustrated
by Bettina Guthridge

Southwood Books Limited
4 Southwood Lawn Road
London N6 5SF

First published in Australia by Omnibus Books 2000
This edition published in the UK under licence from
Omnibus Books by
Southwood Books Limited, 2001.

Text and illustrations copyright © Bettina Guthridge 2000

Cover design by Lyn Mitchell
Typeset by Clinton Ellicott, Adelaide
Printed in Singapore

ISBN 1 903207 36 3

ITALY

The capital is Rome.

The money is the lira.

57 million people live in Italy.

The language is Italian.

The Italian flag.

MAP OF ITALY

SWITZER[LAND]

Monte Bianco
4807 m

FRANCE

MILAN

TURIN

River Po

GENOA

CORSICA

SARDINIA

CAGLIARI

MEDITERRANEAN
SEA

AUSTRIA

SLOVENIA

VENICE

BOLOGNA

PISA

SAN MARINO

River Arno

FLORENCE

SIENA

Tiber River

ROME

Mt Vesuvius

NAPLES

POMPEII

ALBEROBELLO

STROMBOLI

PAESTUM

LIPARI
ISLANDS

Mt Etna

SICILY

N

W   E

S

3

Italy is in southern Europe. It looks like a long boot sticking out into the Mediterranean Sea.

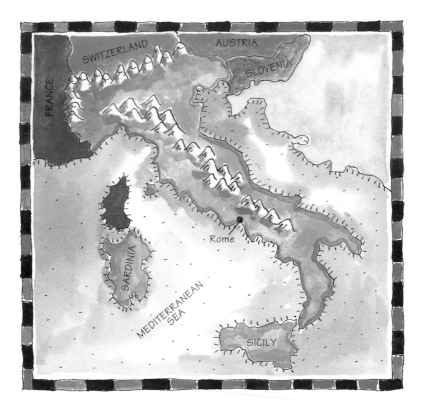

To the north of Italy are France, Switzerland, Austria and Slovenia.

A chain of mountains runs right down the middle of the country.

In Italy there are mountains and volcanoes, lakes and beaches, and glaciers and hot springs.

The islands of Sicily and Sardinia are also part of Italy.

Sicily and Sardinia are the biggest islands in the Mediterranean Sea.

People go to Sicily for holidays. Some towns are built on top of high, rocky cliffs. To get to the beach, you have to take a lift through the cliff.

Sardinia is rocky and very windy. Some people who live there have small farms.

During winter shepherds live in the hills with their sheep. To keep warm, they have pumpkin skins full of wine and wear sheep skin coats.

There are three active volcanoes in
Italy. Mount Etna is the highest.

A volcano is a hole in the earth's crust.
Hot, melted rock called magma
expands and rises up from inside the
earth. Rock and gas burst out of the
volcano. This is called an eruption.

When Mount Vesuvius erupted a long time ago the lava and ash covered a whole town called Pompeii. Many people were buried alive.

Today you can see Pompeii and even the casts of people who were buried.

1. People were buried by lava and ash.

2. The bodies rotted away, leaving a space. People poured wet plaster into the space.

3. When the ash was chipped away the casts were left.

This picture was found outside a house. The words say "Beware of the dog".

In the north of Italy there are big cities.
There are many people. Tourists come
to see the art and old buildings.

Jobs are easy to find and most people
live well.

MILAN   FLORENCE   VENICE

In the south it is hard to find a job. The climate is hotter and the country is not good for farming. Southern Italy has poor soil. There is less industry.

Fewer tourists come to visit.

NAPLES   PAESTUM   ALBEROBELLO

In Italian cities, most people live in
small apartments with no garden.

Children must go to the park to play.

In the morning people work or shop for food at the market. Some Italians go home for lunch and a siesta. Shops open again in the late afternoon.

There is a lot of traffic in the cities. You can tell what city a car is from by the letters on the number plate.

MI – Milan   BO – Bologna   Only Rome has the full name.

In the country people live on small farms. Here they grow grapes for wine and tomatoes for sauce. They also grow olives to make olive oil.

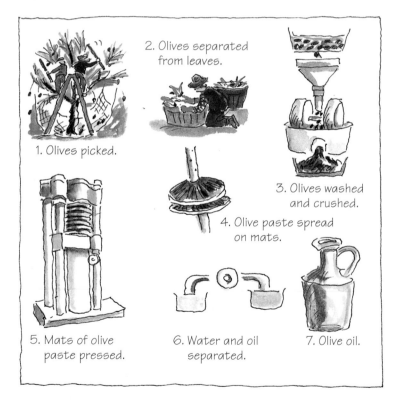

1. Olives picked.

2. Olives separated from leaves.

3. Olives washed and crushed.

4. Olive paste spread on mats.

5. Mats of olive paste pressed.

6. Water and oil separated.

7. Olive oil.

It takes 5 kilograms of olives to make one litre of olive oil.

Wine, tomatoes and olive oil from Italy are sold all over the world.

There are many small villages in Italy. They have narrow, winding streets made of cobble stones. In some places people still use donkeys to carry heavy goods.

small vineyard for wine

olive trees

Tomatoes and sweetcorn dry in the sun.

The family car is often a motor bike with a cabin built over.

Houses in the country look old. Inside they often have new marble or tiled floors. Some farm houses even have a dishwasher.

shutters to keep out the sun

grape vine for shade

Wine, pasta, pizza, bread and most other foods are made at home.

Italians like to eat outside in the summer. Coffee is an important part of the day.

All over Italy there are very old
buildings. There are fortresses, striped
churches, bell towers and domes.

Many towns were built on the top
of hills.

They had huge walls around them to
protect them from attack.

San Gimignano near Florence once
had 72 towers. Rich families built the
towers to show how powerful they
were. Today some are still standing.

Family life is very important to Italians. They also love to eat out. After a noisy lunch, Italians enjoy a walk together. This is called a *passeggiata*.

Italians use their hands a lot when they talk.

Italians say hello with a kiss on both cheeks.

Men like to stroll arm in arm.

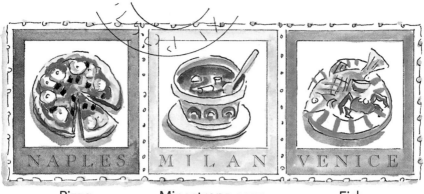

Pizza   Minestrone soup   Fish

Each part of Italy has its own special dishes.

Pasta with meat sauce   Parmesan cheese   Gelato

Italy is famous for its pizza, pasta and gelato.

Long ago, only the rich could have gelato. Slaves had to carry ice from the mountains to make it.

tortellini

cannelloni (big canal)

Flour

Water

Eggs

Italians eat pasta every day.
Pasta is made from special
flour and water and eggs.
It comes in over 350 different
shapes.

Olive oil

Cheese

Tomatoes

A tomato sauce for pasta is
made with olive oil and
tomatoes. Parmesan cheese
is grated on top.

spaghetti

ravioli

penne

farfalle
(butterflies)

ditali

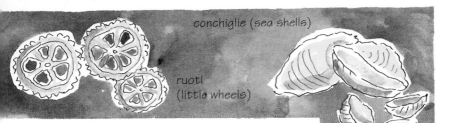
conchiglie (sea shells)

ruoti
(little wheels)

Pasta from Italy is the best in the world. This is how it is made in a factory.

1. Flour and water mixed to form a dough.

2. Dough rolled out.

3. Pasta dough made into shapes.

4. Pasta dried.

pastina

rigatoni

lasagne

cappelletti
(small hats)

The capital of Italy is Rome. Many years ago Rome was the centre of a huge empire. Rome and its emperors ruled many lands.

Cloth and hunting dogs from Britain

Pottery and wine from France

Olive oil and wine from Spain

Wild animals, slaves, wheat and papyrus from Africa

BRITAIN

FRANCE

PYRENEES

SPAIN

ALPS

Rome
Pompeii

MEDITERRANEAN SEA

AFRICA

N
W E
S

The Romans built fine ships. They sailed to far away places and brought goods back to Rome.

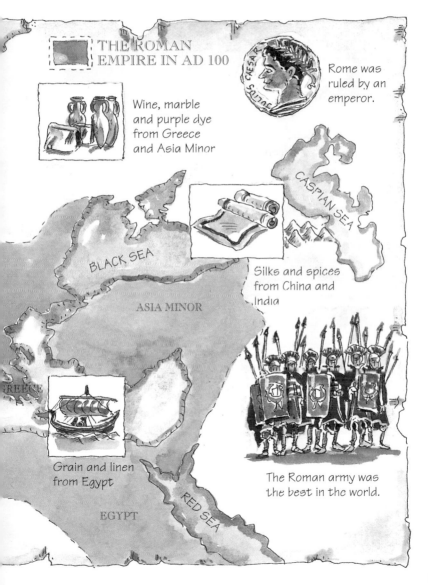

THE ROMAN EMPIRE IN AD 100

Wine, marble and purple dye from Greece and Asia Minor

Rome was ruled by an emperor.

CASPIAN SEA

BLACK SEA

ASIA MINOR

Silks and spices from China and India

GREECE

Grain and linen from Egypt

RED SEA

EGYPT

The Roman army was the best in the world.

Water flowed along the top of the aqueduct in a deep channel.

When aqueducts had to pass through hills, shafts were dug into the hill. Workers dug tunnels both ways from the bottom of the shaft.

The Romans were great builders. They built houses, temples and roads.

They invented bridges called aqueducts. These carried water from the mountains to the cities.

Water for houses was carried in huge pots. The pots were called *amphorae.*

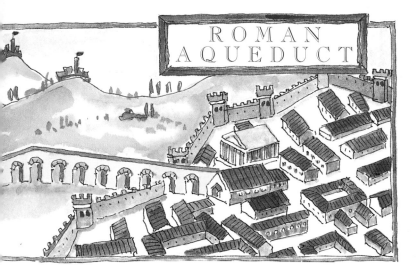

The Romans learned how to build
arches in stone. These were very strong.

This is how the Romans made an arch.

The Romans invented
concrete. They mixed
water and lime and
ash from volcanoes.

The Romans were famous for their games. These were held at the Colosseum in Rome. Here 50,000 Romans watched their favourite sport.

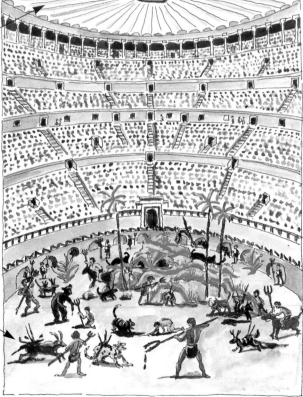

On hot days a canvas cover was pulled over the arena.

Wild animals were lifted by ropes from cages under the arena.

Slaves called gladiators were sent into the arena to kill wild animals or to fight each other.

Wild animals were shipped to Rome from Africa and India.

Gladiators fought animals.

Animals fought animals.

Gladiators fought each other. Many were killed in one day at the games.

The Romans used letters for their numbers. We still use these numbers today on our watches and clocks.

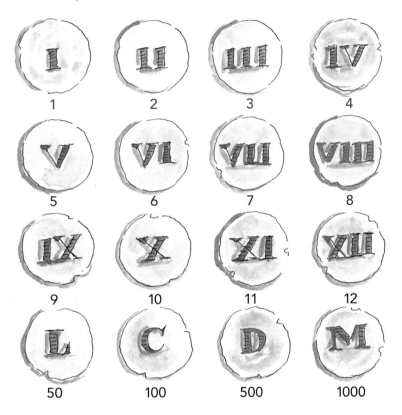

1	2	3	4
5	6	7	8
9	10	11	12
50	100	500	1000

Our calendar comes from the Romans. The months are named after Roman emperors and gods.

The month of August is named after Emperor Augustus.

The ancient Romans spoke Latin.
This language is still written down.

Students can learn it at school.

In Roman times only rich children went to school. They wrote their work on a flat piece of stone or wood called a tablet. It was covered in beeswax.

Students scratched words into the wax with a pointed stick called a *stylus*.

After school children played football with a pig's bladder blown up like a balloon.

In Italy now, children go to school every day except Sunday. Young children wear a shirt over their other clothes as a uniform.

Older students ride motor bikes to school.

Today soccer, volleyball and basketball are the most popular sports.

In the north of Italy is the city of
Venice. It is built on many islands
in a lagoon and has canals
instead of roads.

A bridge for cars and
trains connects Venice
to the mainland.

Venice
Lagoon

car park

port for
ships

In Venice
people travel by
gondola, by a water bus
called a *vaporetto* or by water taxi.

When you die your body goes to the cemetery by gondola.

Grand Canal

ferry

St Mark's Square is very famous.

GONDOLA   VAPORETTO   WATER TAXI

This is how a palace in Venice was built.

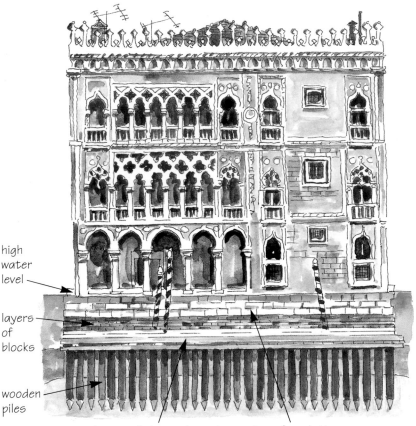

high water level

layers of blocks

wooden piles

layers of clay and sand   stone foundations

Venice is slowly sinking into the water. It is built on timber logs that support stone and rock. These timbers are settling down into the mud.

Many buildings now lean over.

The first people to live in Venice were fishermen. The land was swampy, and so they built their houses above the water. This is how they did it.

1. They made a platform by covering a layer of rocks with planks.

2. They drove long tree trunks into deep parts of the sea bed. Planks were laid on top.

3. The planks were covered with stone blocks stuck together with concrete.

Venice is often flooded when wind pushes the sea into the city. People must walk on high platforms during the floods.

In Italy there is pollution from cars,
factories, tourism and littering.

Rivers are often dirty and clean
beaches can be hard to find. There
is often rubbish on the ground.

Italy did not have laws to protect the
environment until recently.

Laws about buildings have not always been followed in earthquake zones. Buildings have collapsed and killed many people.

Italy has many old buildings and paintings and statues. These are famous and must be protected. Tourists come from all over the world to see them.

One famous building is the leaning tower of Pisa. It was built on soft ground and so it leans over.

Air pollution from cars has damaged many old buildings and statues.

In some places statues have had to be moved inside to protect them. This will help to stop them decaying even further.

Some cities have now banned cars from city centres on Sundays.

On Sundays in Rome the streets are full of people, not cars.

The Italians call Rome *Bella Roma.*

It is a beautiful city full of history.

The Vatican

Sistine Chapel

Castel Sant'Angelo

Spanish Steps

Trevi Fountain

Pantheon

River Tiber

Tiber Island

Colosseum

Roman Forum

A Roman wall encloses the old city.

Millions of tourists visit Rome each year. Many come to see the Vatican.

The Vatican is another city inside the city of Rome.

The Pope lives here. The Pope is the leader of the Catholic Church.

Catholic priests from many countries come to Rome. They pray with the Pope at his church.

The Vatican has many art treasures.

St Peters is a beautiful church. Its large dome can be seen from many places In Rome.

The Vatican has its own flag, money, number plate for cars, stamps and newspapers. It also has its own army. The Swiss Guard protects the Vatican.

The Castel Sant'Angelo has a secret passage to the Vatican. The Pope could go there if he was in danger.

The Pope's window

On special days the Pope speaks from his balcony in St Peters Square.

Most Italians are Catholics. They believe that Jesus Christ, a man born 2000 years ago, was the son of God.

Catholics believe that it is important to live a good life. They believe in Heaven. This is a beautiful place they will go to when they die.

In Italy there are many beautiful statues, buildings and other works of art.

Hundreds of stray cats live in Rome. People feed them.

Michelangelo and Leonardo da Vinci were two of Italy's most famous artists. They lived 500 years ago. Michelangelo spent four years lying on his back painting the ceiling of the Sistine Chapel in the Vatican.

The *Mona Lisa* is the most famous painting by Leonardo da Vinci.

Leonardo also made drawings of huge flying machines.

Some of the best known cars in the world are made in Italy.

Ferrari cars are built by hand by special craftsmen. These cars have won the Formula One Grand Prix many times.

Ferrari 308 GTS

Traffic jams are so bad in Italian cities that many people own a motor scooter as well as a car.

Motor scooters can go to places where cars cannot go.

The baby Fiat (Bambino) is perfect for squeezing through narrow streets.

Cycling is a passion in Italy.

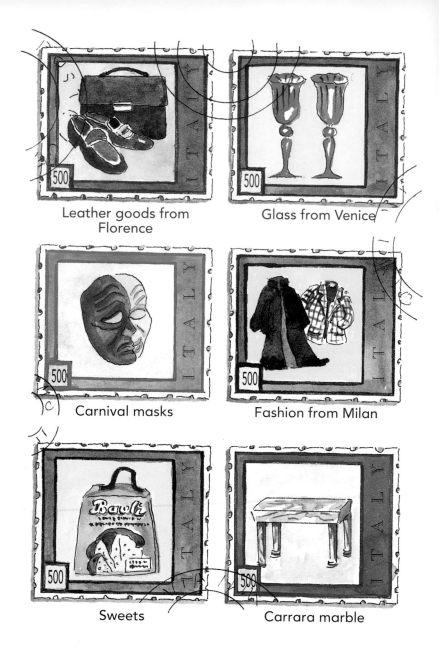

Leather goods from Florence

Glass from Venice

Carnival masks

Fashion from Milan

Sweets

Carrara marble

Beautiful things made in Italy are sold all over the world.

Italian design is
very famous.

The Vespa
scooter is seen
all over Italy.

Giambattista
Bodoni designed
a typeface that is
still used today.

Bialetti is the
name of an Italian
coffee maker.

Italians love to hunt. Now many animals are extinct. Today there are reserves in Italy to protect wild life.

Each year tourists come to Sicily to see the killing of schools of tuna fish.

WILD BOAR   BROWN BEAR

Wolves are part of Roman history. In an old story it is said that the city of Rome began with two brothers called Romulus and Remus.

They were left in the forest at birth. A wolf found them and cared for them.

H A W K   VULTURE

The piano was invented in Italy. The way music is written down is another Italian invention.

The Italians invented opera.

Italy has many famous singers.

The best violins in the world are made in Italy.

Music is heard everywhere in Italy –

along the Grand Canal in Venice,

in restaurants,

on the streets and from the bell towers.

SARDINIA

A statue is carried through the town.

FLORENCE

People parade in costumes.

COCULLO

The statue of the local saint is covered with live snakes.

Every Italian town celebrates its own festivals. The carnival in Venice lasts for ten days. People dress in masks and wonderful costumes.

Italians have a great respect for the land. They celebrate it with many wine and food festivals.

Jousting on
horse back.

A living chess
game is
played on the
town square.

La Befana is
a children's
festival at
Christmas.

Many festivals honour the Virgin Mary
or a local patron saint.

The *Palio* is a famous bare back horse
race around the main square of Siena.
Each rider wears the colours of his
district.

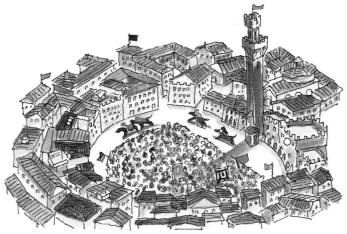

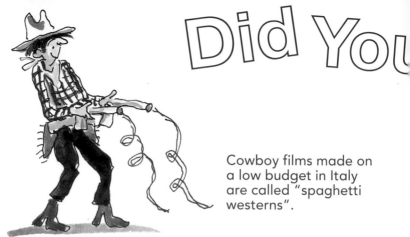

Cowboy films made on a low budget in Italy are called "spaghetti westerns".

Julius Caesar has bad breath

XI

)) **XII**

Meeting at Nero's IV

The walls of Ancient Rome were covered in graffiti.

In Roman times many people shared toilets. Laughing and chatting, they caught up on the latest news.

58

Know?

If you throw a coin into the Trevi Fountain in Rome your wish will come true.

Some people believe that by wearing a piece of coral in the shape of a horn, you can ward off "the evil eye".

In Rome there is a stone mask called "the mouth of truth". Romans believe if you put your hand into the mouth it will be bitten off if you have told a lie.

A wild dance called the *tarantella* is said to cure spider bites. *Tarantella* means "tarantula", a kind of spider.

GLOSSARY

amphorae ★ jars used to carry water.

ancient Romans ★ people who lived in Rome over 2000 years ago.

apartment ★ flat or unit.

aqueduct ★ bridge that carried water.

arena ★ place where games were held.

canal ★ water way dug to carry people and goods between two places.

Colosseum ★ the biggest arena in Rome.

emperor ★ Roman ruler.

eruption ★ explosion of hot gas and rock from a volcano.

extinct ★ died out.

festival ★ a time to celebrate and have fun.

gelato ★ Italian ice cream.

glacier ★ river of ice.

gladiator ★ man who fought in Roman games.

gondola ★ boat with one oar, used in Venice.

graffiti ★ drawings on a wall.

lagoon ★ salt water separated from the sea by a low sand bank or island.

Latin ★ language spoken by ancient Romans.

lava ★ cooled melted rock from a volcano.

linen ★ cloth made from a plant called flax.

magma ★ material inside a volcano.

market ★ place for buying and selling goods.

opera ★ play where the words are sung.

papyrus ★ material to write on, made from reeds.

pasta ★ Italian name for noodles.

pizza ★ dish made with bread dough covered in a sauce and cheese and baked in an oven.

Pompeii ★ ancient town near Naples destroyed by a volcano.

Pope ★ head of the Catholic Church.

shepherd ★ person who looks after sheep.

siesta ★ rest time in the middle of the day.

tarantula ★ a kind of spider.

INDEX